Bonny Cassidy | Chatelaine

New Poems

GIRAMONDO POETS

Bonny Cassidy | Chatelaine

First published 2017
from the Writing & Society Research Centre
at the University of Western Sydney
by the Giramondo Publishing Company
PO Box 752 Artarmon NSW 1570 Australia
www.giramondopublishing.com

Designed by Harry Williamson
Typeset by Andrew Davies
in 10/16.5 pt Baskerville BT

Printed and bound by Ligare
Distributed in Australia by NewSouth Books

National Library of Australia
Cataloguing-in-Publication data:

Cassidy, Bonny, author
Title: Chatelaine
Bonny Cassidy

ISBN 978-1-925336-45-0 (pbk)

Look out the window. And doesn't this remind you of when you were in the boat, and then later that night you were lying, looking up at the ceiling, and the water in your head was not dissimilar from the landscape, and you think to yourself, "Why is it that the landscape is moving, but the boat is still?"

DEAD MAN (DIR. JIM JARMUSCH)

Nature is a language, can't you read?

'ASK', THE SMITHS

Contents

Green and gold wren

We take our gold leaf dose, half half—me and another wife. The phone is off its hook. Read and spell. Tie on a knife, plate, pick and spade; we flit away, low.

Chatelaine

Beware the heath
of wilful words:
an analytic grave.
I prefer the garden plot

where airs live in my ears;
a trowel to dabble
the ponds of peat
that hang beneath the cott.

Morning rakes with me
through moss, diamonds,
pale undersides
that hang beneath the cott.

"Oh the secrets of the bog."
I prefer the garden plot,
where airs live in my ears.
Beware the heath.

Midway along the reddish path.
Midway along the reddish path:
a healthy young noodle
and a happy wee goose come trolling;

monk-free at last, and mutually assured.
"Oh the secrets of the bog."
Lame swards gobble
whorls of rain. The two pilgrims

shimmer on the heath,
noon passing
through moss, diamonds,
their pale undersides.

I get that inner wiggle –
gagging over my trowel –
the low ghost spoofs from me

towards the darling lovers—
I sing it back "Miss Prishen!"

I get that inner wiggling.
I sing it back "Miss Prishen!"

But the wanter has turned their heads
with its muddy poems and they listen
they listen to the multiplying riddles.

Lame swards gobble whorls of rain.
I am polishing my hoard, digging.

Here I am and here I drink.
Sit down and taste my meat,
say what I am called.

Yield and forgive

On her complicated ocean
a fold: tongue, lid
or mountain tip, an ex-life
attends loudly

Oyster perpetual

And who else owns your body

the right way up

is it
the lowland

nude as a needle
where they heard the sun cut in two

away off the map
where they returned
through the eye

bred or bored
speckled

onto crossways
the lusty dregs, well

glazed in seams and rings
it is the hands of cress close

trees deaf under the ice

and pebbles thick as bees

Tropes

She made this place. The parade is lazy, filthy:
to a park as to a country; streets block up swelling
and fat children deliver flags.

There'd be no place without her; no fat park or
livery parade, and certainly no filthy, lazy children
blocking the streets of the country with flags.

We've got her to thank for it all—the block of
fat, its lazy delivery of children to the country,
the filthy park that flags the place down and gets
her swollen.

Treatment (walk-on)

In this poem he yelps from a bailed-up coach,
watched by a dog on the hill.
Then wakes, draped over his brother
in a slop of muslin, screaming for hire.
Damaged, he takes other forms:
a sapling kissed by a child; a sketch
of the prince. He nearly disappears
as a ball of peonies on a sideboard.
When he returns to the poem it's pouring
drinks and he removes his top. Next
he's a cake with ears, a pianola.
In the final lines he multiplies, and they
(different sizes) stand there
viewing the fight.

Sink

this warning
to our gully
where the emus ram
malls of uncoupled think.
Under easy homes and dread
stem, drag the noisy secret
the marble halls.

Dunes

Sweeping the past
out

sounds a gamelan

—

As we crunched from a party

above the river
our heads were trains

twisting oil out of a leaf, she said
why do you always do this

—

You trail it with you
other paths move through
its minute landscapes
more here there
in bed its edges
screech

—

An owl had flown across the mouth
of a river, from burning palms

at dawn

I hunched beneath its scan

concealing the rabbit

—

A condom packed with sand
stood tight and porcelain
creasing on the ledge.
We towed our bikes high to witness it
split in the tide

—

Sleep produces a distant version
of the nearby ocean

I go running in masses to shore

and tunnel in the opposite direction
shaking through the first wave, its remaking

boughs of horizon, the ring

of us before the second wave
and third—a ring loosens

we no longer see one another.

Dry arms on the dipping raft

—

Your voicemail
as I come into range
your voice asking me to move south
as I carry to the lake

across its orange cries

—

In the background clouds
ate each other

my mother demonstrating
meals of beach and air, pouring, pouring

Ex-territorial

Like a stag brought down by two large greyhounds –
whereby they inch and tear
at its forelocks till the whole thing ends in a pile –
the dance pings through my thigh.

Blue birth. Wish. Target
an active transmission
of my unwearying hollowness.

No longer a woman I am, at last, dalek.
Without a skull inside, my gaudy relic
would be revolting. Tis pity you will know
before it rattles out of me:

under these horsey waves, is a graph of rods
in which I shorten to a sharp, cold idle.
All my rivulets of pomp n petal
are simply grated-on. Arch droid. Mantis.
Watch this, now, I'm really going somewhere.

Interior

Her massive smog hinges through his tinder, some
female fry a script that writes itself. She can
hear the sharply dented air around this guy.
Here comes her poem.

Meanwhile the basement carpark fills with liquid
spread thin as mirror turning; discandied
images drift, open-mouthed to the entrance,
signs wade in and cruise.

Inland

I lay my thought
over the bough

mouthless
clear as confidence

its spiral
tipped and
drawn.

I will imagine you in foreign streets;
not at the feet of history
but in the alley where it limps.
Sometimes you
come back in drips
from your shoulders, other eyes.

Last light mine
I stand up in the field

incommensurable

a doric winter
straight
my fluted brain.

Spermicidal

Wherein his escape from the house is quite unghostly *(Sir is that you Sir?)*

At the corner she picks him up in her cab, wheezing; his
sorrowful bells cling. Tonnes of her alive in the underpass.
Backseat, he peeks into his cup: two barren eggs, two actresses.
The imperatrix accelerates

and, through some cosmic flushing, mr rococo
the pervert packs off to the north

Nether

It stood, sweating
pages of ash.

—

Stretched days stare
from the ridge.

I roam into their lights.

—

My fingers hook and unhook.
Listening to voices
flutter up the cliff and long bottles of flame explode.

The track lies
back, shadows sleep through.
Turn it all upside down.

—

You were young then

floated

and might have come with me to the sunken creek.

Now I bend
reflection flattens me
apart.

Now everyone has fire
they sit.

—

Embers jump from my mouth,
weeks collapsing.

The moon flies on.

—

I've cut the evening

        my face locked
        one eye at a time.

—

The warm dimensions of mist
move with me;
storming breaks ahead

and I brink forward, off the plateau.

Do you have any idea

—

Over itself the river's drag
firm. Ascent

from paper soft with stench and thwack
of current hurtling.

—

If a thin touch
spells out
upriver

already I've passed you
(the bank's brave, first star)
rising myself in time.

—

My last face was tripped
with open water, buds caught in its
mouths.

—

Swamp bedding.

From its pattern
I separate
each blade clear—
no myth, I dredge
the polis of moss in my ears.
Slowly twisting trunks
crash to cinders.

——

Spine unlike smoke.

——

The whole year is stripes
and grids of appetite

wash away the surface,
eat it through.

——

Into the apartments of sand
I entered flat under the door.

——

Night tightens its grip.

I rust

boiling
mineral blue.

How to be both

Hard-edged hothouse and sad young man.
How to put hair on a rock; glisten bits, trinkets.
To cut the muscle cycle, oyster-mouthed,
and exit fanny-first. Stinking pitch. Ribbons.
I want to look like this.

Slow news

Memory is a spotlight:
faces grow on trees,
kangaroo shoulders tense;
in the American library, arms of wattle.

Faces grow on trees:
poet and followers on the arms of the couch
in the American library, arms of wattle.
People resemble trees often.

The poet and followers on arms of the couch:
birds of prey find stamina in government
and people resemble trees often, they say;
here is yesterday's camel.

Birds of prey lose stamina in government:
a mist with no healthy heart.
Here is yesterday's camel—
false doors to the beautiful west.

A mist with no healthy heart:
memory is a spotlight—
like false doors to the beautiful west,
kangaroo shoulders tense.

The red studio (moveable types)

Father was a potted fern, reclining miner, a diadem.
Moth' went in sheepskin, sweet camouflaged poison.
Sap trembled from my armpits.
We reposed in panoramic undergrowth
clutching our mild expectations.
Spooks flew.
Behind curtains, the boulevard looped.

Pancake

Listen

later you'll be born, and younger
fully made, asking how soon
until you're a window sill.
Wherever you squint will be
just before or just after. You
may not become an urn; may be
praying and praying for nothing
a bit of Zola can't make true.
That's the horror of the hamlet:
no tits, but your outfit can
depict tussocks leaning on crystal.

Schwärmerei. I remember
my heart when Inga's silver name
got sprayed up the library wall.
Who cares where love comes from?
asks a kid running past the end
of this letter and into your same.

Axe derby

Never were knuckle-men.
Choked up on planks

of smoke, they haul
towards the peplum, stabbing

back at time, splinters of it
flip like cars. Rolled sleeves,

knees cooked, the rousie
is flirting with her broom, a blonde

with criminal simplicity with
historical truth we can detoxify

a poisoned planet. Now
they're descending the spirit heap

dribbling pinkies along fair knotty thighs.
Children are returning to pick up the butts.

Still the brunette is caving in the face
of time, is making herself a living

treasure from this surplus
hour the minutes fly

Puff puff

You could lug the feeble creature forever.
It trudges in your arms, trailing over fence and curb.
Its tassles shiver.

Green panic

Hungry grass is cursed grass: biding its time, barely
working it sees them unload. Wispy woke us, beating back.
It came, invited

gimping, juicy heads aloft. Its nipples, barbed and
jammish, will feed the villa's dog. They'll knock at the
verandah, full of fibre; they know what they're doing
and the horse they rode in on.

Now our villa was empty and they felt good with their
slabs up on the sofa. A raid beaks through the windows,
harrumphing in the space. *She's an old idea, he's not invited:*
the strangers say it with glances. Off on off.

But they didn't love it so they left, and through the dust,
worms turning. Dawn a language of circles and nods.
The suburb approaches on castors; they've called a
scorched hearth gorgeous.

Juvenilia

When he's very

his sister nearby always,
her face rests on his back.

The boy lies doggo.
Lush in the dark

tailing burrs like strewn

cuckoos lift their knees, shake
craws and soon

he takes bark
for skin—the watcher's

gushing
through his shoulder.

(Detail)

Pieces of city unfinish on the plains,
flames at their gutter. Kestrels rev
as a hairy hand reaches through their path and
calmly stacks the skidding dust.

It monologues a touch; we chew the facts, nodding.
We get in beneath its raspy nails and calmly work
into the body the system, light tapers and pass them around.

Nightwork

A conveyor belt reaping into action, cries

rubbish rocks rubbish rocks

breaks up floodlight, its flesh
a stingray covered, uncovered.

Pandanus leans
magic, enters the bulldozer
rearing
its tyres dissolve

as from the rocks and rubbish
the camera conveys

one kid
naked and furiously sweeping
a path through reeds, pandanus
shaken
entranced

by the trucks and manganese
at her feet.

The old men spin like tyres covered, uncovered.

It's the sixties, then it isn't.

Shut-eye

In my best version she
nails a headland
between my bronzers
and I slump to the ceiling
grinning claws
going tat tacky tachy:

Dreamboat

/

Here we are
in a big aeroplane
with its lounge, its silently
snapping fire and cut glass

/

In a dream my brother
I mean sister died
and I delayed grief, offering it to others
first. It was politeness
and eventually I turned see-through.

The next day I spoke to her
on a screen. He'd been crying.
The screen remained solid
looking

/

When you lose something in a dream
it falls to the bottom, swiftly rattled
out

but you won't think of going back
to beat through acres of mid-air
prowling the distance

/

We sense that soon
the aeroplane will land,
and go about swapping seats.
But the plane's really more a boat
which rather than landing
will only continue to buff and displace molecules.
It banks and banks

/

In a riverbed I lay

three sleeps of clawed cobalt

and on the fourth, a sand-blank expanse
filled up behind my lids.

Prints forming round the dry bend

/

The dream doesn't narrow into a tube;
it shreds

like an elderly pencil, it reverts—

you turn it upside
to begin again (the phantom of a pause)

/

You can't find your seat
so you crouch along
the forest of rows:
it's right at the back
of the forest, which has gone
dim and tonal.

The plane floats on,
a day above night

Cathexxxis

She met her official husband as he strode
off from his inland schoolhouse. Since then
she has only ever heard the first three words
of his sentences. Over his shoulder she sees
the boy, playing dead like a mango …

All the misplaced fauna has driven the boy
to dance—a spirit of his own device, coasting
through her oblongs and nobody's business.
The magpie goose he brings
is a metaphor swinging from her reach.

Signifiers turn to pulp outside the window.
There's enough moonlight for the boy to see in,
where the ants are resting on her sighs. She rarely
listens, preferring to know his lines take shape;
panting, pretending it's a vocal exercise.

She hardly think about her parents:
the present is her country while it lasts.
Ochre doesn't think of brick. Besides,
nothing happened and no one believed them—
a flight of asses from the paperbark.

The shot buffalo jumps up.
… Over her shoulder, the husband ponders
his next wife emerging from the harbour
and all those legs going walkabout in the city.
They hover like this beside Elizabeth Bay

where she put down her knife.

Sick in the head

The nineteenth century clicks
round the plaza, a spring-loaded pigeon.
Stone on frumpy stone puckers

at his boots
through the hordes—

defaced men beware

his cherried shield
not quite crimson
it talks

to them in their own language, it walks
like Werther, their rosy neighbour

but it's Fanta-Face, they whisper
here it comes

he
the

– Amerika –

comes now
asking for coffee
the women staining themselves with brown bread, hello

come his women in men, his men in magenta

Ditty

Ladder of bombs, you
make your tracks forth
trickling from that bitch of sea.

And come to me a gentle
stiff, soft in weeds
I peel like a century.

The past gaping up at us
from the sand; you lantana me rain.
Nature, lack, because, whatever.

The rest is hissy, chill
shrines clot the headland.

Lighten up

I blow in by dark, from the other spot.

The water statics into very deep places
of the unsightly thing—stolid as a wart.
It could be dead, I guess, or frozen. Its silhouette is strewn
like dunetops, unfaithful.

Doing the hag, I offer the thing
favours for a sip. It seems to accept. I load it with my fleshly garb
then lean in.

I once loathed this corner of the village, it was so wreckable with
its downturned eyes. The thing carried pools of defunct currency,
tweens stole its dollars and hurled them into the nearby ocean.
Animals avoided its transparency, staring at the vacant arches.

Now its eyes have been fucked out, as the villagers say,
and the offshore wind pumps through them, into my hair.
Close up, the thing improves—triangulated and useful,
like exhumed lumber, stirring.

I arrange old gum and tickets around its lips, and drink.

Before they come to hoist me away, above the barren
thing, into branches over the bay.

Thick mirror

Bolt soft/bush glass/tear

mat/bent black/flash teat/thin mass

low peak/ripple shot/limp cot/rubber

bulb/flipper tint/crack yam/bright

roots/short blink/back

box/sharpen streak/

sliver work/digitd

rop/wrinkled sham/

mistik crap

Mostly water

In winter the garden
is the back of our head

a faint young sun.

By morning the house
has forgotten much of it.

—

Last night I caught you
reading strands from the plughole

pointing to the shrunken stranger
crackling in the tumble-dryer.

I thought of my grandmother pointing
proudly past her daughter's shoulder
to the photograph of her daughter.

—

The rain rises fast.

I'm wondering what my young girl's doing
now, and what if

she were faintly real.

I've made you aware
you'll never know.

—

When you quiz the electronic mind
she doesn't listen,
and as you sleep
I break her up
into neat sticks.

Let them lie.

—

You wake

our hydrogen bonds.

I'm mostly water
as you know.

You're saying how warm you feel
trying to scrape off my sweater
like an energetic young son.

—

The rain huddles

removes its feet.

Acquittal

The squire was on His Tour Of Tears.
She rowed into town and read the superscript of pastness on its tiles. Elsewhere foundations had been glossed by the ebb. She fingered idears like loaded bricks or single strokes of grass filtring through the floodplains. Coolabahs floundered in the blanky blank as she barged to His deserted headquarters.

Hunt

Crowds flee
every beat of your noncreamy heart against
its body of skyscrapers.

Blocks away men are waiting
to cop rays off its windows,
or they loiter inside it—lost there for years
craning upwards.

As you plod home they dip
between your steel paws just to keep up, voices
tapping on glass.

Somehow you fit through the front door, somehow
eat and sleep to scale
woken by another naked intruder unzipping
from your pencil case—

Dad phoning the police and heating up milk
saying, now you're fourteen.

Stump, trunk and can

Your torso parked against a salmon gum.

Or, you as a terrified hero-horse, chest
ground against the earth.

You made by fat, drastic thumbs
and a squiff of zinc for your fag end.

Now you're a bastard
you might as well dress as one
and eat the meat that bastards eat.

The distended spider hanging
from a mosquito coast, its network of tails.

The bear at the centre of the colosseum.

You as teal-coloured, graven
with signs of delta: whiplash, eel and parvenu.

The cup with two saucers.

Your shin as a boot that rests
while the body tramps on.

You as a hull fading into view.

Planed by the rush, sockets thrown,
your face coming away in my hands,
an anchor

falling through streets—pausing
to lick the page awake
muffled in the crotch of a long gaze.

DIG

In the pan your gravels crashing hatched their prize—
a brindle rush to hump my veins and fever up the leaf
that twisted in our fields. The guilt was white, my soul a sieve
It boomed with bull to see the dust an avenue of spin—and
my brickhouse hazy as a reef, its aura built to scale. I seemed
to tap its skin. Birth was the pits but this is mine. Rabbits
swimming to shake my mitts.

Floored

Mam draws the clock down
with her eyes
asks me gently.

Knuckles blanching I work from her nape
to the ball inside the shoulder.

Lunch rings a little bell—
my fingers blink

across the table her tread
yells shadow.

Dropping
her nightdress darkens;
she never drowns but makes another cliff.

Spunkie

Look at the lip on your innards:
you thrive on drunks. So
what misorder drove you here?

What holly-follow, dangling you
all the shortest day—what pseudo
voodoo draped
you over yourself
twice

and logged
your nippy snout, cracked—a little
smiling clog.

What, rippling
at the door of the mire?
What was green and king.

Sessional

This seems a nice hollow, but too many places have been
ruined by pissing in or on.

Over time and the rim of your faultless comma, you will
pretend to see nothing nothing nothing—neither the fried
nuggets nor tanned hide of the front bar's gruntlings.

A tragedy executes angles (an incline and a decline, in
which the final fortunes rest lower than they commence);
a poem travels across them.

First spend the money and then to sea.

Be careful what you chuck out, it might have meaning
to someone.

Be more strict with your pussy; reserve for three or four,
you, and only for frigging.

Sink your slipper in.

Your darlin phase begins (honk) with changing colouration:
large slim brick, to incinerette. Like a keg of ale, it's a
common wolf-trap used by a lesser kind of woman.

Consider the warm melancholy of an
unaccompanied painting with its abandoned action.

Question nearly everything, read it again.

Two piece (deleted scenes)

Lifesize clouds of the present
zoom

behind them
in the dicky sky

unsashed, rain:
rich and worthless

strips the crowded horizon.
A suburb of islands bends

aching in silhouette
its face a canoe

a pallid method
now wait for the page to harden, furniture

to pop—roiling
pips sparkle in the sand and me

with my clods of fuzz,
simple.

Half virgin

Ants pour out and in.
A teensy voice, a child in a well
whose horse has stalked off.
And who, caught there
in her funnel of notions,
sews up sentences.

Women and men come by
with the wrong roses,
standing outside the slit
sniffing. Each ant is
a note; her
compositions seep
in and out of sight.

National vegetable

Bom bom bony road
its heads of boy
his pipe and folded throat.

Feedly om and rest.

A squall that yammering
hoard of empty coins

collect.

Tub tub the maiden
prangs her cans no
mouse a pony in its fur.

Catch up mots.

Sop sop heartland
and what it knows:
the raging lake of genes

some hills had teeth now.

The parade reels back so
bom that pony shucking bom
through estate embers bom bom

Madam

Fancies strike me in the
overflow like men
who all look the same

come over and disappear:
ravines suspended across a bridge.
That bird walks downstairs, an oyster

eating another. I spits up poems. Please
torch these thoughts like cash, help me finish the vase
then shatter it.

Destiny

The duck is sceptical

agape
it faces the deep
passing time.

The duck sighing
shuffles
its beak

writes the word
blame.

Study of a man's right shoulder, breast and upper arm

His unguarded rainbow, barbarian skies.
Bold, the line that touch her not

(the girl with titian flare,
a haunch of man.)

His gown turns copper loosens
as a squid. Cherubs confiscate his things.

Saints do paint
but not themselves—

the unconscious is Roman.
A distant flick of sheep like maggots.

The nerves in his quiver
hatch their way
to a fond coup

the public disappears below in a fateful haze

(and behold, I come quickly).

The host

Dusk surged.
In a fit of despond, he went back to the party
and stood with puddles of lily-folk.
They whipped the fog of old regret—
a neverending udder he dimly groped for hours
like storytime, and sucked it up,
like daylight fussing.

The way you live

The middle is low tied
I hear, a trough that rips.
Blokes march out to the middle.
In the middle is the verb
flying towards
and flocking. As I circle
the middle it tries to sag.
The tiny car in the middle.
The artist making herself from fluff.
I swallowed a tiny car once;
it remains parked inside
where the lies begin, small
pyramids of salt. A glass age.
Without talking about the middle
I am in it, making a case for myself.
Where running turns to ruins.
From here the middle
is flat as joy as trodden wax.
They might have died in the middle.
The middle has a rounded base
and in the middle are two square holes
the way back in.

Hot mess

All is rendered less, with
quivering tines pricked
above a sock of heat:

dishy, this one – crammed
with history, stuck –
and how its cheek is full.

Foams that lay before
turn soggy and, worse, triple-sweet.
Carve, Jane, carve—or pass

and think of words until
your perfect mound arrives.

Sheila

Down below
the milepost dressed
in a rope gown

through granite, fishes

the oil-dark boy grasping
a goldy fist.

Under a fig of sweat
he parts himself

the gnawable vacancy
where his cheese petrifies

into a bowl of meaning.

Go suckle there, see
your image surf to you.

Entrance (1988)

Strains of gutworthy
crescendo onto your
chenille, medium tide –
eyes brassing the verge –

as you scrape
a leafless pool
where soon you will bob,
broken mast, chicken
and white wine breathing.

Blason

Now, poets
rehearse for us
]
]

that musky terror
whose frights were forgot
already long ago
]
hearts chant.

"Up the scrub she hurled
a grey cat, rising
her pall pout hounded and true

Oaks hatched scant
as a big fink's pubes she pedalled
a storm of next coming.

]
Our veins shook. The pond filled with prams.
]

'Look, brothrs! A stunner'd
crush her magic with his stone book
were there martyrs here to teach

]

But youse hide in leaves
watching that breeder grasp and
]
faster through our woods of stunted fancy.'

Still as her silky hunches clipped
on wheels, pups struggled in slipshod
leathers, white panting strained the stitches
of her stringless motley

]
became a wiff of faint and heels
creaked, vaping far into the forest
hanged like pelts."

Come, rats
]
and as the poets retch and keen
we jangle our dags

]
we undig our burrows
]
]

Moods (wet dream)

When she rove strategic
high and fast, she know you at length

unrolling your attention as if by foot.

And say she
drop closer (unmoved breasts, your yellow kiss)
inhaling a clump
of feathers, cardboard, lost sprigs

will you
have she
all the way around. Step back
anytime she want.

She pay the creek's wages
she climb inside.
Plumes distended, a bundle of she
watches from a cystic rock.

Lie down all the time she want.
In bellbird notes your litter

airy blood she eat
and gather pecks of honeysuckle
for your monument

walking once about
she, your only mate

Invisible idiot

Shoving loam aside, the roots are writing
THE QUEEN DIED.

He travels the virtual grassland in his soft machine,
overtakeless. This is the country of shutup listen and observe.

He knows the roots are repeating themselves
AND THEN THE KING DIED.

Their memory is filling, untranslated; beneath his feet

squirm chunks of its helpless data, wiring patterns of
VEGETABLE ABUSE and DOWN WITH IMPOSSIBLE LOVE

Arete

Here am I again in you: crimped
edge to edge a constellation,
like Ajax whose passion plunged
into itself. I wake to the split
of your back on my mind.
Contrapposto I wake –
a personification of the vine –
from a scene inlaid with rotting
youth, its words evaporated and
wheeling open like a plate.

Research

Cut that strap and fall to the stupid
nightmare someone else
invented for you.

Burning cheery on the town square.
Born again a pearl.

Even now you don't say everything;
go to your endless childhood
and stand in the trees, waiting to kiss.

Now the strands on a silent film, or a record thudding.

Walk the castle wall
on the shallow bay out
beyond the fringe of nation.

Through the subfusc distance sluts
in their bloomers roast chops.

Key-fumble
away from his symbols,
keep gathering rocks.

Acknowledgements

Earlier versions of several poems have appeared in *Axon, The Age, The Australian, Plumwood Mountain, Cordite Poetry Review, Overland, Rabbit, Snorkel, Island, Zone* (UK), *Splinter* (UK), *Tender* (UK), *Blackbox Manifold* (UK), *Poetry* (USA) and *Burning Bush 2* (Ireland). Thanks to the editors of these journals.

'Entrance (1988)', 'Yield and forgive' and 'Shut-eye' were originally written for *Dear Everybody*, an ekphrasis project featured at the Emerging Writers' Festival 2015.

Thanks to Alice Allan, Luke Beesley, Leah Muddle and Robert Wood, who helped me to draft parts of this work. Gratitude to Tim Grey and Matthew Hall, who read versions of the whole.

These poems were made on the lands of the Kulin, Gunditjmara, Jardjwadjali, Ngunawal and Yuin peoples. My respects to their elders past, present and future.

The Giramondo Publishing Company acknowledges the support of Western Sydney University in the implementation of its book publishing program.

This project has been assisted by the Commonwealth Government through the Australia Council, its arts funding and advisory body.